Barbara McClintock: Pioneering Geneticist

Kathleen Tracy

Mitchell Lane
PUBLISHERS

PO Box 619
Bear, Delaware 19701

Unlocking the Secrets of Science

Profiling 20th Century Achievers in Science, Medicine, and Technology

Barbara McClintock:
Pioneering Geneticist

JB
McClintock
Tracey

First Printing

Library of Congress Cataloging-in-Publication Data
Tracy, Kathleen.
    Barbara McClintock: pioneering geneticist/Kathleen Tracy.
        p. cm. — (Unlocking the secrets of science)
Includes bibliographical references and index.
Summary: Presents the life and career of the geneticist who in 1983 was awarded the Nobel Prize for her study of maize cells.
    ISBN 1-58415-111-0
    1. McClintock, Barbara, 1902—Juvenile literature. 2. Geneticists—United States—Biography—Juvenile literature. [1. McClintock, Barbara, 1902- 2. Geneticists. 3. Nobel Prizes—Biography. 4. Women—Biography.] I. Title. II. Series.
    QH429.2.M38 T73 2001
    576.5'092—dc21   2001044404

ABOUT THE AUTHOR: Kathleen Tracy has been a journalist for over twenty years. Her writing has been featured in magazines including The Toronto Star's "Star Week," *A&E Biography* magazine, *KidScreen* and *TV Times*. She is also the author of numerous biographies including "The Boy Who Would Be King" (Dutton), "Jerry Seinfeld - The Entire Domain" (Carol Publishing) and "Don Imus - America's Cowboy" (Carroll & Graf). She recently completed "God's Will?" for Sourcebooks.

PHOTO CREDITS: Cover: Cold Spring Harbor Laboratory archives/Herb Parsons; pp. 12, 18, 29, 40 Cold Spring Harbor Laboratory Archives; p. 30 Photo Researchers; p. 36 AP Photo/Bookstaver.

PUBLISHER'S NOTE: In selecting those persons to be profiled in this series, we first attempted to identify the most notable accomplishments of the 20th century in science, medicine, and technology. When we were done, we noted a serious deficiency in the inclusion of women. For the greater part of the 20th century science, medicine, and technology were male-dominated fields. In many cases, the contributions of women went unrecognized. Women have tried for years to be included in these areas, and in many cases, women worked side by side with men who took credit for their ideas and discoveries. Even as we move forward into the 21st century, we find women still sadly underrepresented. It is not an oversight, therefore, that we profiled mostly male achievers. Information simply does not exist to include a fair selection of women.

3065200110042

Contents

Barbara McClintock, a 20th century Mendel.

Chapter 1

The Way We Are

• •

Over the course of history, the human quest to gain scientific knowledge has often been severely hindered by the human reluctance to accept new knowledge. Whether out of fear of the unknown or resistance to new ideas or even because of politics or religious beliefs, people aren't always willing to encourage or listen to freethinking individuals. Many people who are now famous for their discoveries were virtually ignored during their lifetime.

Gregor Mendel is a perfect example.

For hundreds, even thousands of years, it seemed obvious from simple observation that parents passed on many of their physical features and traits to their children. Generation after generation of one family would be born with a particular body type or with a certain color of eyes or some other feature. And while some children may look more like their mother while others look more like their father, overall they appeared to be a unique combination of both parents.

However, nobody knew exactly how this happened or the nature of the mysterious process that passed along these family traits. It wasn't until Mendel devoted seven years to studying pea plants that the mechanics of heredity were first understood.

Mendel was born in 1822 into a farming family in what is now the Czech Republic. Because their son was such a brilliant student in school, his parents encouraged him to pursue his education rather than come back to work on the family farm. But they didn't have much money, so Mendel entered a monastery in 1843 and took religious vows four years later to become a priest, all the while continuing his education.

Perhaps because he had grown up on a farm, Mendel loved nature. He was fascinated by the theories of evolution, studied meteorology (the science of weather) and had a keen interest in plants. It was while he was strolling around the grounds of the monastery that he combined two of his favorite areas of study—plant life and heredity. To him, science was everything in the world around us. It was endlessly fascinating and, most of all, exciting and interesting. '

In his first experiments, he grew two different types of plants next to each other to see if just being alongside another kind of plant would cause them to exchange traits. It didn't. Every generation of plants retained its distinct traits, unaffected by environment or nearby plants. So if plants changed, it had to be because of something inside of them.

Next, Mendel turned his attention to pea plants. At first, he crossbred different varieties just "for the fun of the thing." But over the course of several plant generations, he noticed that there seemed to be a mathematical ratio to certain traits. Some traits seemed to "dominate" others, either in color or leaf variety.

Out of this observation, Mendel set about to prove the idea he had formed about why this happened. Between 1856 and 1863 he crossbred thousands of pea plants and eventually developed the first basic laws of heredity: hereditary factors do not combine, but are passed intact; each member of the parental generation transmits only half of its hereditary factors to each offspring, with certain factors "dominant" over others; and different offspring of the same parents receive different sets of hereditary factors.

In 1866, the year after the American Civil War ended, Mendel published *Experiments with Plant Hybrids*, in which he described how traits were inherited: both parents contribute material that determines the characteristics of their offspring. But his theories were virtually ignored and quickly forgotten by the scientific community at large. They would remain lost for the next thirty-four years. As has happened so many times in science, his ideas were so brilliant and unprecedented that people simply couldn't— or wouldn't—believe him. More than that, they didn't even take him seriously.

It didn't help that the one scientist who responded to him gave what turned out to be very bad advice. That scientist suggested that Mendel should continue his experiments, but use hawkweed, a different plant. Because hawkweed reproduced itself in a different way than pea plants, the data Mendel collected was worthless and he became discouraged.

In addition, he became the abbot, or leader, of his monastery in 1868. That kept him so busy that he had no time left over for research.

Fortunately, though, time has a way of balancing things out and eventually Mendel's theories would be accepted as fact and the monk would become known as the "father of modern genetics." He not only changed the way we see the world and ourselves but also the way we live in the world.

Sadly, Mendel died in 1884, long before his theories were accepted and hailed for their importance so he never knew the impact his work had. But to him, notoriety and fame weren't what mattered; the importance was simply doing the work and trusting that people would eventually come to see what he saw.

Although he couldn't have known how important his observations would one day be, Mendel's work eventually became the foundation for modern genetics. His explanation of heredity was especially remarkable because it was based only on visual interpretation of breeding experiments, long before the mechanics of cell division were even discovered.

Just before his death, he said, "My scientific labors have brought me a great deal of satisfaction, and I am convinced that before long the entire world will praise the result of these labors."

That belief in the work, and believing in oneself regardless of what others may say or think, allowed Mendel to persevere and ultimately be proved right.

And it was those same qualities that would keep Barbara McClintock working in near obscurity for forty years, pursuing her own scientific theories and beliefs, often in the face of skepticism and ridicule. In the end, she, too, would be proven right. But unlike Mendel, she lived to see her work receive the recognition it so richly deserved.

Gregor Mendel's work with pea plants formed the basis for the modern science of genetics.

As a young woman, McClintock attended Cornell University.

Chapter 2

Ahead of Her Time

• •

Barbara McClintock was born in Hartford, Connecticut on June 16, 1902, the same year that aspirin was invented and Marie Curie won the Nobel Prize for physics. Her mother, Sara, had come from a wealthy and socially prominent family who could trace their origins in this country back to the pilgrims on the Mayflower. Her father, Thomas, came from a more modest background.

When they met, Thomas was a struggling medical student with very little money. But Sara was an independent thinker, especially for that time, and didn't care that Thomas wasn't from her family's elevated social class.

Early on, Sara had shown she wasn't afraid to do things her way. After her mother died when she was a baby, Sara was sent to live with relatives in California. But as she grew older, Sara longed for the more cultured world of the East Coast. So she hopped a train and traveled cross-country all by herself to go back to Massachusetts and live with her father. She eventually met Thomas, fell in love with him, and the couple were married in 1898. Once again showing her forward thinking, Sara even helped her new husband finish medical school by paying his tuition out of her own money.

Early in their marriage, the McClintocks moved around a lot while Thomas struggled to get his medical practice going, even though they had started a family. Barbara was their third child and when she was three she was sent to stay with her aunt and uncle. Her uncle was a fish dealer and little Barbara would climb on his horse-drawn carriage every day and go to work with him. When her uncle bought a car, Barbara would try to help him fix it when it broke down. Even though she was away from her parents, she would recall this period as a wonderful time in her life.

In 1908 Barbara returned to her family. Tom and Sara had finally settled in Brooklyn, New York, where they raised their four children: Marjorie, Mignon, Barbara and the baby of the family, Malcolm, who everyone called Tom. Even as a little girl, Barbara was the most like her mother—adventurous and filled with curiosity.

Naturally, Sara encouraged her daughter to be independent and self-sufficient. Barbara would recall to Evelyn Fox Keller, author of McClintock's biography *A Feeling for the Organism*, "My mother used to put a pillow on the floor and give me one toy and leave me there. She said I didn't cry."

As she grew up, Barbara wasn't like the other girls she went to school with. Instead of wanting to participate in activities such as sewing and cooking that girls were expected to like, Barbara preferred to read, play baseball in the summer and ice skate in the winter and, as Robert Henry recounted in the book *Her Heritage: A Biographical Encyclopedia of Famous American Women*, just spend her time "thinking 'bout things." She also was passionate about science.

Somewhat surprisingly, though, this made her mother Sara a little uncomfortable. She was worried that her daughter wasn't feminine enough and, according to Henry, might become "a strange person, a person that didn't belong to society."

On the other hand, Thomas and Sara McClintock were raising their children in a way that many people might have considered strange. For one thing, Barbara and her siblings were all urged to develop a variety of interests and not to let their education begin and end in school, but to let the world be their classroom. Thomas made it clear to the children's teachers that he didn't want them saddled with homework at night, believing it was better that they used their time finding out about other things in their lives.

Even when she was young, Barbara realized she was different from other kids her age, especially girls. She liked climbing trees and playing sports and just staying active, which sometimes caused her to be made fun of. She admitted to Keller that "I found that because it was not the standard conduct, doing as I like might cause me pain. But I would take the consequences for the sake of an activity I knew would give me great pleasure."

While Barbara enjoyed physical activity, she was also a good student and managed to graduate from Erasmus Hall High School when she was just sixteen years old. However, neither of Barbara's parents expected her, or even wanted her, to pursue any kind of higher education. For as freethinking as they were, the McClintocks still held the common attitude that a college education wasn't really proper for a girl.

When Barbara finished high school in 1918, young ladies were expected to look forward to marriage and having children, not to pursue higher education and especially not a career. Although women in America had been allowed to run for political office since 1788, it wouldn't be until 1920 that women were granted the legal right to vote. Most men—and many women—genuinely believed a woman's place was in the home. And even those women who thought differently didn't have a lot of choice in their lives because there were very few jobs available to women.

Still worried that her daughter was growing into a "strange person," Sara also fretted that her daughter was perhaps too smart and that if she went to college, young men wouldn't want to marry her because she was more intelligent than they were. More than anything, Sara worried what would happen to Barbara if she never found someone to marry. Being a single woman at that time usually meant a life of poverty and loneliness.

Barbara, on the other hand, did not share her mother's well-wishing concerns. What did concern her was that regardless of her desire to go to college, she might never be able to afford it. Even though her dad was a doctor, the family was not wealthy. When World War I broke out in Europe and Thomas was required to go overseas for a few months to treat wounded soldiers, the family's financial situation got worse. Sara gave music lessons and Barbara got an office job to bring in some money. But even though her dream of going to college seemed more impossible than ever, Barbara refused to give up hope—or give up learning. When she wasn't working at her job, Barbara spent her free time in the local library, learning as much as she could on her own.

Eventually, though, Barbara figured out a way to go to college even without any money. When her father came back from Europe, she told him she wanted to enroll at Cornell University's College of Agriculture because there was no tuition—they educated their students for free. As independent as she was, Barbara needed and wanted her parents' approval, otherwise she wouldn't be able to go.

Finally, Thomas had a change of heart. He convinced his wife that Barbara deserved the chance to follow her dream, even if it was out of the ordinary. He believed her passion for learning was a special gift that should be supported.

So in 1919, Barbara McClintock enrolled at Cornell University. She craved to learn why things happened in nature the way they did and couldn't wait to start her classes. Not only was Barbara smart, she was also outgoing, a lot of fun to be with and had a good sense of humor. So when she wasn't studying, Barbara enjoyed hanging out with friends and enjoying college life. She even played banjo in a campus band and was elected president of the women's freshman class, even though she may have seemed a little odd to some of her classmates.

Whereas other girls followed the current style and wore their hair long, Barbara cut hers short. She also dressed for comfort rather than fashion, choosing to wear pants instead of skirts. And she didn't spend time worrying about whether or not she would ever get married. Although, much to her mother's relief, Barbara began dating in college, she never became involved in a serious romantic relationship. Years later she would comment it was because she never let her friendships with other people distract her from her studies and work.

During her first few years at college, Barbara took a variety of courses, always enjoying what she was learning but still unsure what she wanted to devote herself to. But it wasn't long before she would take the class that would determine the course of her life.

Barbara worked long hours with maize in her laboratory. She examined individual kernels and recorded all her observations.

Chapter 3
The Secret Life of Corn

• •

At the end of her junior year Barbara was invited to take the graduate course in genetics and was unofficially made a graduate student. Although she wanted to study plant breeding, school officials thought that was not a suitable subject for a woman. In fact, that department refused to accept any female students, so McClintock registered for botany instead, which was considered an acceptable field of study for women at the time. Her major was cytology—the study of cell function, formation and structure—with minors in genetics and zoology.

In her autobiography, Barbara said, "By the time of graduation, I had no doubts about the direction I wished to follow for an advanced degree. It would involve chromosomes and their genetic content and expression, in short, cytogenetics. This field had just begun to reveal its potentials."

Although most women who studied science went on to become schoolteachers rather than to pursue careers in research, Barbara had no desire to stand in front of a class. She wanted to be on the front lines in the laboratory, discovering the mysteries of inheritance.

Two years before Barbara was born, Gregor Mendel's groundbreaking theories about heredity had been rediscovered and confirmed by three scientists named Hugo de Vries, Karl Correns and Erich von Tschermak. Since the time Mendel had conducted his experiments, several major discoveries regarding heredity had been made, giving scientists more pieces of the genetic puzzle. But still nobody completely understood how all the pieces fit together.

In 1868, Fredrich Miescher, a Swiss biologist, successfully isolated nuclein, later called DNA. But it would be a long time before anyone would understand the connection between DNA and the laws of heredity described by Mendel. That someone was Walter S. Sutton. In 1903 he published *The Chromosomes in Heredity* which stated that genes—inherited bits of information that control an organism's traits—discussed by Mendel were actually contained inside cells on structures called chromosomes. Sutton's paper was one of the first to make the connection between genetics and the biology, or physical makeup, of a cell.

Even though Mendel's work had now been accepted as fact, there were still many details about heredity genetics that remained unclear by the time Barbara began working towards her Masters Degree in botany in 1923. In fact, scientists couldn't even agree on what exactly a gene was. Today we know that a gene is a unit of DNA that controls a particular trait. We know that chromosomes are groups of coiled strands made up of DNA and proteins and that we get half our genes from our mother and half from our father. And that's true whether you're a plant, animal or person.

Thanks to Mendel, we know that some of the traits we inherit are dominant, or stronger, and some are recessive, or weaker. An example is whether we have hairy or smooth knuckles.

So, any time the dominant gene for hairy knuckles (written as a capital H) is present, whether both genes are dominant (HH) or one gene dominant and one recessive (Hh), that person will have hairy knuckles. However, if children inherit the recessive gene from both parents (hh), then they will have smooth knuckles.

But back in the 1920s, all this information was still in the process of being discovered and understood, which made genetics an incredibly exciting field of study for someone like Barbara, who loved solving what to her was a puzzle. And it didn't take long for her to show others her skills at observation.

During her first four years in college, Barbara had enjoyed taking a variety of classes, dabbling in a lot of areas that interested her. But once she started graduate school she discovered a surprising passion for corn. And not just any corn, but a type called *Zea mays*, more commonly known as maize or Indian corn. Unlike the kernels of regular corn, which are either yellow or white, maize kernels differ widely in their coloration.

At the time, Cornell University had the best department of maize genetics study in the country. Barbara worked in the laboratory of Rollins Emerson, the dean of the graduate school, who was considered a top maize geneticist. Like Emerson, she found maize the perfect plant to work with and wasted no time unraveling some of its genetic mysteries.

She spent countless hours looking at cells through her microscope and developed a special ability to prepare slides of cells for view under the microscope. Slide preparation can be tedious and is painstaking because the specimen, in this case from the corn cob, needs to be sliced thinly enough to be able to see the cells and dyed with stain so the cells stand out.

But the most important talent is to be able to understand what exactly it is you're seeing. Barbara had a knack for seeing things other people couldn't—which is how she made her first important discovery during her very first year in graduate school, although that discovery wouldn't please everyone.

As a graduate student she first worked as a paid assistant to Lowell Randolph, a cytologist who had been appointed to a position at Cornell supported by the US Department of Agriculture to work with the maize geneticists and—it was hoped—strengthen the maize plant breeding efforts.

However, McClintock and Randolph did not get along well and soon dissolved their working relationship. This was because Barbara managed to solve a question that Randolph had spent much of his career trying, and failing, to solve— finding a way to tell the ten maize chromosomes apart from one another. Part of the problem was unreliable staining techniques, as well as the fact that the chromosomes in the root tip material generally used for such studies could not be reliably distinguished. McClintock solved both problems.

From all her hours looking through the microscope, McClintock noticed that there were subtle but distinct differences in the ten chromosomes. Some absorbed the stain she used differently, some had little bumps or knobs located in certain areas, and there were slight differences in length from chromosome to chromosome. Barbara was looking at the same thing that countless others, including Randolph, had seen through the microscope but she was the first one to observe the differences. As a result, she quickly learned to tell the ten chromosomes apart by how they looked. She also developed a new staining technique that allowed her to tell which chromosomes carried a particular trait. Although today it seems like a minor achievement, it was a stunning accomplishment at the time—especially for a woman student.

In an online account, Nina V. Fedoroff says McClintock's colleague and lifelong friend Marcus Rhoades would later comment that even though Barbara and Randolph did not get along, "Their brief association was momentous because it led to the birth of maize cytogenetics."

Like Mendel had done with his pea plants, Barbara needed to raise her own maize in order to keep careful notes and records on which traits were inherited from which parent. But growing corn is a little more difficult than growing pea plants and Barbara spent much of her time in graduate school out in the fields. Sometimes, she felt more like a farmer than a scientist!

Although some people might have wondered why learning about maize was important at all, Barbara understood that unlocking the secrets of genetics in maize would provide knowledge which could then be used in many different ways. For example, animal breeders might develop better cattle and farmers could grow more robust crops. This would help to increase the supply of food, not only in America but also around the world. It could also help doctors understand different diseases and perhaps come up with cures.

Although Barbara just wanted to understand maize better than anyone ever had, she realized that in many ways unlocking the mysteries of maize genetics was the key to unlocking the secrets of life itself. What could be more exciting than that?

Barbara spent much of her time cultivating her Zea mays cornfield, but she also made time to teach her findings to students.

Chapter 4
An Unexpected Finding

• •

In nature, corn is normally pollinated by insects or by the wind carrying the pollen from the part of one corn stalk called the tassel, to another stalk's silks, long strands of hairlike material. But in order to study the genetics of her plants in a controlled way, Barbara McClintock needed to make like a bee. So she manually took the pollen from one stalk's tassel and pollinated another stalk's silks herself, which is called cross-pollination. Then once the corn was ripe, she'd pick the ears and go back to her laboratory to study the results and share them with her colleagues.

Among the other students working in Rollins Emerson's lab was George Beadle, who would go on to win the Nobel Prize in 1958 for his work with enzymes, the chemicals that speed up chemical reactions in the cell and are necessary for life. But when Barbara knew him, he was just a fellow graduate student working alongside her. Years later, Beadle and others would admit they had often been amazed at her powers of concentration and observation.

"She was so good!" Beadle was quoted in Mary Kittredge's book, *Barbara McClintock*. Another student, Marcus Rhoades added, "She was something special. I've known a lot of famous scientists but the only one I thought really was a genius was McClintock."

So did a lot of other people. Barbara impressed so many people in the scientific community with her discoveries that even before she finished her education she was considered a pioneer in the new field of maize cytogenetics—

the analysis of genetic occurrences in corn cells—which for the first time provided a visual connection between certain inheritable traits and their physical basis in the chromosome. For example, she realized that the color patterns of a particular corn cob's kernels corresponded to differences of the cob's cells when looked at under a microscope.

After she finally earned her Ph.D. in botany in 1927, Barbara was offered a job as an instructor at Cornell. She accepted the job because it allowed her to continue her work with maize while earning more than enough money to support her modest needs.

Although teaching wasn't a particular passion of Barbara's, some people thought that she was a natural educator. Biologist Tom Broker of the University of Rochester told Robert Cooke of *Newsday*, "She taught by asking questions. She was full of insight and very dynamic."

Another friend, Howard Green, observed on the website www.nalusda.gov that Barbara could also be a demanding instructor who believed students should be expected to perform their best with little help. "'Let them sink or swim!' she used to say," Green recalled.

In 1929, Barbara met a new graduate student named Harriet Creighton. The two women hit it off immediately and soon Harriet was assisting Barbara with her maize experiments. These experiments were now focusing on meiosis, a special form of cell division that happens only in gametes, which are the cells involved in reproduction. In meiosis, the cells split apart twice so that each gamete has only half the number of chromosomes as the parent cell.

For example, each maize gamete has five chromosomes. But when two gametes unite, the offspring has the full ten chromosomes. The same process happens in animals and people. That's how you get half your genes from your mother and half from your father.

Sometimes genes that lie very close to one another on a chromosome tend to be inherited together. These are called linked genes. Barbara wanted to show in her experiments that during meiosis, occasionally some of the chromosomes exchange or transfer genetic information, a process called crossing-over. This would explain how linked genes could become separated so the traits are no longer passed along together. Although simple sounding, it was a revolutionary idea because up to that time it was believed that genes were arranged on a chromosome sort of like beads on a thread, stationary and unable to move.

Using a set of chromosomal markers McClintock had discovered, she and Harriet proved the relationship between chromosomal crossover during meiosis and the separation of formerly linked observable traits. Even though they had amassed enough material to leave no doubt as to their findings, Barbara hadn't gotten around to presenting the results to the scientific community at large. The way that scientists usually present their findings is to publish an article but Barbara was hesitant—until she got encouragement from Thomas Hunt Morgan, one of the most famous and respected scientists of his day. Back in 1910, he had conducted experiments with fruit flies that proved the first correlation between a specific trait and a specific chromosome, which became known as the chromosome theory of heredity. Many genetics studies after that were built on Morgan's findings, including Barbara's.

Morgan was at Cornell as a visiting lecturer and was naturally interested in hearing about the research currently going on. When he heard about McClintock and Creighton's results, he urged them to publish their findings as soon as possible. Fortunately, Barbara and Harriet listened to his advice and as a result, got the credit for being the first to prove that crossing over occurred during meiosis.

Writer Richard Robinson recalls how when a colleague once marveled at her ability to see so much simply by looking at a cell under a microscope, McClintock replied, "Well, you know, when I look at a cell, I get down in that cell and look around." She went to say about chromosomes, "I found that the more I worked with them, the bigger and bigger they got, and when I was really working with them I wasn't outside, I was down there. I was part of the system."

It was her ability to concentrate that allowed Barbara to actually imagine herself inside the cell and look for answers to her questions. "As you look at these things," she said, "they become part of you. And you forget yourself. The main thing about it is you forget yourself."

A year after publishing "A Correlation of Cytological and Genetical Crossing-over in *Zea mays*," Barbara and Creighton presented their findings again, this time in front of five hundred scientists at the International Congress of Genetics. Although McClintock had no desire to be the center of attention, thanks to her work she was already considered one of the top scientists in her field and her presentation at the conference just added to her reputation. But fame meant very little to McClintock and despite her growing fame, the thing that still mattered the most to her was her work. "I did it because it was fun," she said in the magazine *Earth Explorer.* "I couldn't wait to get up in the morning! I never thought of it as 'science.'"

And as it turned out, Barbara McClintock's greatest discoveries were yet to come.

McClintock was an individual thinker who preferred comfortable clothes over the fashions of the day.

Adolf Hitler's harsh politics shocked Barbara and caused her to cut short a Guggenheim Fellowship research trip to Berlin.

Chapter 5
Jumping Genes

• •

By the time she was thirty, Barbara McClintock was internationally famous within the world's scientific community because of her discoveries. But despite all her accomplishments, Cornell University would not offer her a professorship because at the time women simply weren't hired for that kind of high-level teaching position. And McClintock had no desire to languish as a low level instructor. Luckily, in 1931, she had been awarded a fellowship from the National Research Council and used the money to support herself while trying to figure out where she should go next to continue her research.

For a while she spent time at the University of Missouri, where she hooked up with one of her old Cornell colleagues named Lewis Stadler. Stadler asked her to examine the chromosomes of some plants that had been zapped with X-rays and ended up producing offspring with mutations and other abnormalities. Barbara discovered that the X-rays had damaged the chromosomes in a variety of ways. In her mind, she could see that the chromosomes might actually break apart, then join back together in a ring formation. Again, the idea was revolutionary but many other scientists believed it was true simply because Barbara said so.

But that wasn't good enough for McClintock so she set out to prove her theory. Mary Kittredge's book *Barbara McClintock* reveals that Barbara was nervous that she might be wrong. "I got scared," she said. "When the plant was opened, my hand was actually shaking. I took it right back to the lab and—it had rings!"

Today, we take for granted the knowledge that X-rays can be harmful to cells but back in the 1930s, this was brand-new information. The importance of Barbara's discoveries cannot be overstated because they propelled the study of genetics in ways nobody had thought of previously.

In 1933, on the recommendation of Thomas Hunt Morgan, Lewis Stadler and Rollins Emerson, McClintock was given a Guggenheim Fellowship to go to Berlin, Germany, where she was scheduled to collaborate with Richard Goldschmidt, a well-known geneticist. But Berlin in 1933 was at a boiling point. Adolf Hitler and his Nazi party had achieved supreme political power. It wasn't until she went to Germany and saw for herself that Barbara realized the depth of the Nazis' anti-Semitic attitudes. Already, many German Jews had fled the country out of fear for their safety, including Curt Stern, the scientist she had barely beaten out with her paper on crossing-over. It quickly became clear to Barbara that this was not a safe place to work or live and she came back to America after only a few months. Goldschmidt also eventually left Germany in 1936 and found haven in America, where he continued his work.

Although McClintock was relieved to be back in America, she had no job or laboratory to call her own. Her old mentor, Emerson Rollins, managed to get her a grant from the Rockefeller Foundation, which helped support her work for another two years. She earned a small salary for working as Rollins' assistant, but mostly she spent her time on her own experiments. Barbara had always been independent and unconcerned about what other people thought or did, but she couldn't help being terribly disappointed that her opportunities were so limited simply because she was a woman.

Eventually, it was Lewis Stadler who came to the rescue. In 1936, he convinced the University of Missouri to offer Barbara an assistant professorship, which she immediately accepted. In the lab, she continued to study chromosomes damaged by X-rays and discovered that broken chromosomes were able to reconnect, or reanneal, to other broken chromosomes. She also showed that broken chromosomes could heal themselves. It's almost as if she were single-handedly reinventing the study of genetics.

But despite her obvious importance to the scientific and academic communities, despite the honors being bestowed on her, such as being elected vice president of the Genetics Society of America in 1939, Barbara still could not be a professor. What Barbara needed was a place where she could settle and devote all her energies to her work. In her heart, she knew the University of Missouri would not be that place. Not long after she had been hired, the local paper printed the engagement announcement of "Barbara McClintock." Even though it was another young woman who happened to have the same name, Barbara's department chairman thought that it was actually Barbara and told her that she would be fired if she chose to get married.

So in 1941 she left. By chance, she happened to write her friend Marcus Rhoades to ask where he was growing his corn that year. He told her he was going to the Cold Spring Harbor Laboratory.

Located in Long Island, New York, Cold Spring Harbor Laboratory was a premier genetics research center that had been founded by the Carnegie Institution. Assuming that it would be temporary, McClintock accepted an appointment to work there for a year. As things turned out, she remained there for the rest of her life.

Life at Cold Springs Harbor suited McClintock. It was private; she was surrounded by other scientists and could work at her own pace—which usually meant nonstop. And in 1944, the same year that McClintock was elected a member of the National Academy of Sciences, she was confronted with a new mystery whose solution become the defining moment of her already brilliant career.

She had noticed that some of the maize plants she was examining had a strange color pattern, with streaks and spots scattered around the kernels. Barbara spent a long time thinking why that could be. Sometimes, she took long walks on the Cold Spring Harbor's wooded grounds, even taking the time to pick walnuts, which she would use to bake walnut pies. Then it was back to the microscope, imagining herself inside the chromosomes looking around.

Eventually, the answer seemed clear—the discolorations resulted from two "control" elements whose location on chromosomes was not stationary. There must be movable elements inside the gene, which she called "transposable elements" that caused the color variations.

In her theory, a "control" could turn a nearby gene "on" or "off," but was in turn controlled by a second element farther away. This main "control" could move from one spot on a chromosome to another, hence the term "jumping genes." For example, if a particular gene's job is to make a corn kernel dark, and the control gene turned it off, then the corn kernel would be light in color. If the control gene jumped away to another position, the gene would be switched on again, and the corn kernel would become darker.

For almost six years, Barbara gathered data and conducted experiments. She finally published her work in 1950 and a year later presented her findings at the 1951

Cold Springs Harbor Laboratory Symposium. It wasn't the first time McClintock had presented revolutionary ideas but it was the first time her conclusions were not only met with skepticism but openly dismissed as ridiculous. Because her work challenged a cemented belief among mainstream geneticists—that genes were fixed in place—her research was rejected. She was deeply stunned and bitterly disappointed at the closed-mindedness of her peers.

But rather than stop her research, she simply stopped telling anyone about it. From that point on, she refused to publish any more papers and stopped giving lectures, concentrating all her energies on her work and meticulously keeping records.

Her refusal to publish and open herself up to more criticism resulted in her falling out of view and to some in the field she became almost a forgotten figure for nearly two decades. It wouldn't be until twenty years later that her theories would be verified when molecular biologists isolated transposable elements in bacteria and discovered that they were used by cells to control genes—the same discovery that McClintock had made twenty years earlier in maize. Suddenly, once again Barbara McClintock, who was now in her 70s, was being hailed as a genius and her work was finally getting the recognition that was twenty years overdue.

During all those years when her work was ignored, Barbara had patiently kept doing research and locking the results away in her files. According to Robert Cooke of *Newsday*, McClintock never once let the situation make her doubt herself. "They called me crazy, absolutely mad at times," she said. "But if you know you're right, you don't care. You know that it will come out in the wash."

Seen here standing beside Dr. Louis Sokoloff, Barbara received the Lasker Award in November 1981 at a ceremony held in New York City. The Lasker Award is the most prestigious prize offered in America for medical research.

Chapter 6

The Ultimate Honor

• •

Now that the rest of the scientific world realized Barbara had been right all along, McClintock came out of her self-imposed cocoon and began publishing paper after paper about transposition—and this time, other geneticists listened. The importance of her work went way beyond academic interest because transposable elements directly impacted our understanding of evolution, not just in people but also in microbes that cause disease.

What McClintock proved was that a gene's structure could change. And usually this was a positive thing. It made it easier for a plant or animal to adapt to its environment, such as becoming more resistant to drought or high temperatures or cold—in short, to live longer. Then when it bred, it would pass this new trait to its offspring so it, too, would have a better chance of surviving longer.

However, for all the positive results jumping genes have had, there's also a down side. Some mutations can result in inherited diseases such as hemophilia. The more scientists learn about how and when genes jump, they might be able to control it and thus prevent many terrible inherited diseases.

Currently, scientists are hoping to create jumping genes in mosquitoes that carry malaria in order to make them unable to transmit the deadly disease. It is also believed that jumping genes may play a part in normal cells turning into cancer cells. It's very likely the day will come when

McClintock's work will ultimately be the basis for saving countless lives.

As if to make up for their mistake in not believing her, the scientific community began heaping praise and awards onto Barbara. In 1981 alone, when she was 79, Barbara won eight awards, including one that guaranteed her $60,000 a year, tax-free, for the rest of her life. The attention, and her sudden wealth, made McClintock extremely uncomfortable. Mary Kittredge quotes Barbara as saying, "I don't like publicity at all. I never wanted to be bothered by possessions or to own anything. Those things have never been important to me. I want to be free of all that. All I want to do is retire to a quiet place in the laboratory. I'm an anonymous person."

Not anymore, she wasn't. And on October 10, 1983, the announcement came that ensured she would never be anonymous again. The entire world learned that Barbara McClintock had been awarded the Nobel Prize in Medicine and Physiology for her work in transposable elements, becoming the first woman in history to win that award on her own without any co-winners. For the next several months, between the announcement and when the Nobel would be awarded, Barbara's life was a whirlwind. But she never got caught up in it and always retained her sense of humor.

Her friend Evelyn Witkin recalled the time McClintock received an invitation to a dinner for Nobel laureates from the famous politician Henry Kissinger. While the invitation listed all the other guests as "Dr.," Barbara was referred to as "Ms. B. McClintock." On the invitation Barbara wrote, "I don't get no respect!"

The Nobel Prize award ceremony took place on December 10, 1983 in Stockholm, Sweden. Barbara attended with the other five winners that year. When it was her turn to be presented with her Nobel diploma, gold medal and check for $190,000 by Sweden's King Gustav, those present greeted Barbara with thunderous, almost deafening applause. Typically, Barbara gave a short speech, barely three minutes in length, and mostly spoke about the joys and privileges of working alone with her maize. As she had commented previously, "It seems a little unfair to reward a person for having so much pleasure over the years."

And equally typically, when the hoopla of the Nobel was over, Barbara returned to Cold Springs Harbor and her laboratory and her corn. Despite all the money she now had in the bank, McClintock lived the same modest way she always had and spent most of her time researching and trying to find out ever more about the nature of genes.

But as she neared 90, McClintock began to noticeably slow down. Although her mind was as sharp and quick as ever, her body seemed to be weakening. Her keen sense of observation was still strong and she told friends she would not live past ninety. And as she had usually been throughout her life, McClintock was right again. She died September 2, 1992 with her friend Joan Marshak at her side.

In the months following her death, tributes poured in from around the world and a memorial in her honor was held in November of that year. Many people noted laughing that it was exactly the kind of thing Barbara would have hated. But her friends and peers gathered to reflect on her legacy to the world of science in general and genetics in particular and to remember the good-humored but intense woman who overcame great odds to achieve all she did.

John Robinson, in Child's Life, quotes McClintock as once saying, "I've had a very, very satisfactory and interesting life. I couldn't wait to get to the laboratory every day," she said. Then she offered this advice to young students who dreamed of being a scientist: "They have to be motivated so they enjoy what they're doing, and, therefore, see what they're doing."

As always, Barbara McClintock's observations were right on target.

Once her work with jumping genes was recognized, Barbara McClintock finally received the recognition, and respect, that had eluded her for 40 years.

Barbara McClintock Chronology

- 1902, born June 16 in Hartford, Connecticut.
- 1908, moves with family to Brooklyn, New York.
- 1915, enters Erasmus Hall High School in Brooklyn.
- 1919, enrolls at Cornell University.
- 1925, identifies the 10 chromosomes in corn.
- 1931, proves crossing-over occurs in chromosomes.
- 1931, is awarded a two-year National Research Council Fellowship.
- 1932, honored at Sixth International Congress of Genetics.
- 1936, appointed assistant professor of genetics at University of Missouri.
- 1942, joins research staff at Cold Spring Harbor in New York.
- 1944, is elected to the National Academy of Sciences.
- 1946, discovers transposable genetic controlling elements in corn.
- 1951, failure at Cold Spring Harbor Symposium.
- 1963, appointed consultant to the Agricultural Science Program of the Rockefeller Foundation.
- 1967, wins National Academy of Science Kimber Genetics Award.
- 1970, awarded National Medal of Science.
- 1981, wins Albert Lasker Basic Medal Research Award.
- 1981, awarded Wolf Prize in Medicine.
- 1981, named MacArthur Prize Fellow Laureate.
- 1982, begins collaboration with Steven Dellaporta.
- 1983, wins Nobel Prize.
- 1986, receives National Women's Hall of Fame Award.
- 1992, dies September 2.

Genetics Timeline

- **1858:** Charles Darwin and Alfred Russel Wallace present theory of natural selection.
- **1859:** Darwin publishes *The Origin of Species*.
- **1866:** Gregor Mendel publishes his research on hereditary factors in pea plants, stating that inherited characteristics are carried in discrete units called genes.
- **1868:** Fredrich Miescher isolates DNA.
- **1900:** Mendel's principles of inheritance are rediscovered, signaling the start of modern genetics.
- **1902:** Walter Sutton establishes the relationship between heredity and cells.
- **1905:** Nettie Stevens and Edmund Wilson determine the X and Y sex chromosomes.
- **1910:** Thomas Hunt Morgan proposes theory of sex-linked inheritance and gene theory.
- **1928:** Fred Griffiths discovers the phenomenon of transformation, by which one kind of bacteria takes on traits of another, although Griffiths doesn't know exactly what material is being passed between cells.
- **1931:** Barbara McClintock and Harriet B. Creighton demonstrate crossing-over in maize.
- **1944:** Oswald Avery, Colin MacLeod and Maclyn McCarty discover DNA is responsible for transformation.
- **1948:** Barbara McClintock develops theory of transposable elements to explain color variations in corn.
- **1950:** Erwin Chargaff discovers one-to-one ratio of enzymes adenine to thymine and guanine to cytosine in DNA.
- **1952:** Martha Chase and Alfred Hershey prove DNA is the basis for heredity.
- **1953:** James Watson and Francis Crick determine that DNA's structure is a three-dimensional double strand helix of nucleotides.

- **1966:** Marshall Nirenberg and H. Gobind Khorana crack the genetic code.
- **1972:** The first recombinant DNA molecules are produced.
- **1972:** Transposable elements are discovered in bacteria.
- **1977:** Genentech, the first genetic engineering company is founded; it manufactures medical drugs.
- **1982:** Recombinant DNA technology is used to synthesize human insulin in bacteria
- **1990:** Gene therapy is first used in humans
- **1990:** The Human Genome Project is begun with the goal of sequencing and mapping all human genetic information.

Further Reading

Books

Aronson, Billy. *They Came From DNA*. Scientific American Books for Young Readers. New York, NY: W.H. Freeman, 1993.

Eisenhart, Margaret A. and Elizabeth Finkel. *Women's Science: Learning and Succeeding from the Margins*. Chicago: University of Chicago Press, 1998

Hacker, Carlotta. *Nobel Prize Winners* (Women in Profile Series). New York: Crabtree Publishing Company, 1998.

Herskowitz, Joel and Ira Herskowitz. *Double Talking Helix Blues*. Cold Spring Harbor, NY: Cold Spring Harbor Laboratory Press, 1993.

Keller, Evelyn Fox. *A Feeling for the Organism: The Life and Work of Barbara McClintock*. San Francisco, W.H. Freeman, 1983.

Kittredge, Mary. *Barbara McClintock*.(American Women of Achievement series). Broomall, PA: Chelsea House, 1991.

Markey, Kevin & the Ladies Home Journal. *100 Most Important Women of the 20th Century*. Des Moines, IA: Meredith Books 1998.

McGrayne, Sharon Bertsch. *Nobel Prize Women in Science: Their Lives, Struggles, and Momentous Discoveries*. Seacaucus, NJ: Birch Lane Press 1993

Sternberg, Steve. "Gene Cuisine on the Menu," *Science News*, March 1, 1997, p. S21.

Travis, John. "A Fantastical Experiment: The Science Behind the Controversial Cloning of Dolly," *Science News*, April 5, 1997, p. 214.

Web Sites

http://www.accessexcellence.org
http://www.nobel.se

Glossary

Allele: an alternative form of a gene. For example, A, B, and O are all different alleles of the blood-type gene.

Biodiversity: the range of variation among all living organisms.

Cell: the smallest, self-contained unit of life.

Chromosome: a grouping of coiled strands of DNA containing many genes.

Cytology: branch of biology studying function, formation and structure of cells.

DNA: Deoxyribonucleic acid. DNA is found in the chromosomes inside every cell in the body and through its chemical messages inherited traits are passed to the next generation.

Dominant: the form (allele) of the gene that appears to dominate or mask another form of the gene when two different forms are present. Dominant alleles are often written in capital letters.

Enzymes: complex chemicals made of protein found in living cells that speed up reactions inside the cell. Without enzymes, our bodies would not function.

Genes: individual particles of heredity; functional units of DNA that determine a particular trait or characteristic.

Gene pool: all the possible alleles for a particular gene (or all genes) within a given population.

Genetics: branch of biology that deals with how an organism passes its traits on to its offspring.

Genome: set of chromosomes of an organism containing all of its genes and associated DNA.

Genotype: the composition of alleles of an organism. For example, a person whose phenotype is type A blood can have a genotype of AA or AO.

Heterozygous: having two different alleles of a particular gene, e.g. Hh for hairy knuckles or AO for blood type.

Meiosis: special form of cellular division that produces cells with half the number of chromosomes as the original parent cells.

Mutation: change or damage to a DNA gene which sometimes alters the genetic message carried by that gene.

Phenotype: observable traits or properties of an organism.

Population: local group of individuals belonging to the same species.

Recessive: form of a gene that is masked by a dominant form.

Trait: observable variation of a particular inherited characteristic, such as eye color.

Transformation: movement of DNA from one cell to another.

Transposable Elements: pieces of DNA that can move from one area of a genome to another, causing mutations.

Barbara McClintock is shown here in 1983. Her story is important for even more reasons than her scientific discoveries. When Barbara was growing up in the early 1900s, science was not considered a proper career for a woman. Throughout the latter part of the twentieth century, women have struggled in the sciences to be recognized for their accomplishments. Barbara is a pioneer among women in science.

Index